Animals of Africa
HIPPOPOTAMUSES

by Tammy Gagne

FOCUS
READERS

FOCUS READERS

www.focusreaders.com

Focus Readers is distributed by North Star Editions:
sales@northstareditions.com | 888-417-0195

Produced for Focus Readers by Red Line Editorial.

Photographs ©: Gudkov Andrey/Shutterstock Images, cover, 1; Photocech/ iStockphoto, 4–5; Red Line Editorial, 6; JMx Images/Shutterstock Images, 8–9; Dmitry Balakirev/Shutterstock Images, 10, 29; spukkato/iStockphoto, 12; GP232/ iStockphoto, 14–15; curioustiger/iStockphoto, 16; GlobalP/iStockphoto, 18; EcoPrint/ Shutterstock Images, 19; Zoran Kolundzija/iStockphoto, 20–21; RollingEarth/iStockphoto, 22–23; Goddard_Photography/iStockphoto, 24 (top); Karel Bartik/Shutterstock Images, 24 (bottom left); Luca Luceri/Shutterstock Images, 24 (bottom right); cabman237/ iStockphoto, 26

ISBN
978-1-63517-265-2 (hardcover)
978-1-63517-330-7 (paperback)
978-1-63517-460-1 (ebook pdf)
978-1-63517-395-6 (hosted ebook)

Library of Congress Control Number: 2017935151

Printed in the United States of America
Mankato, MN
June, 2017

About the Author

Tammy Gagne has written more than 150 books for adults and children. She resides in northern New England with her husband and son. One of her favorite pastimes is visiting schools to talk to kids about the writing process.

TABLE OF CONTENTS

CHAPTER 1

TIME TO EAT!

A group of hippopotamuses wades in the river. The lead hippo grumbles. Other hippos join him. They make booming sounds. They slowly leave the river. It is time for the hippos to **forage** for dinner.

One hippo leads others in search of food.

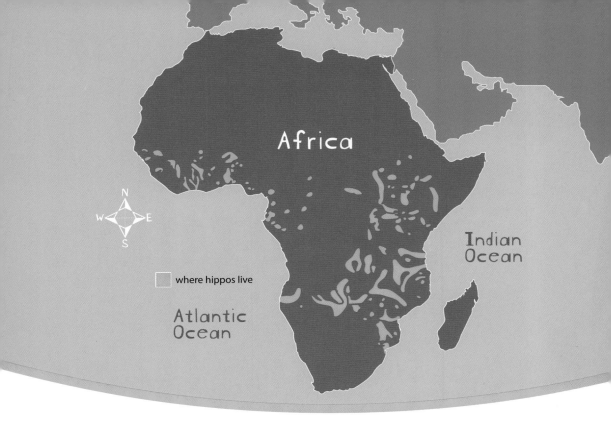

Africa

N
W E
S

where hippos live

Indian
Ocean

Atlantic
Ocean

Hippos live in many places across Africa.

During the day, the air is at its hottest. Hippos are not very active. They rest in the cool water. They spend as many as 16 hours there each day. Hippos must leave the water to get food. Their travels could take them 6 miles (10 km).

Hippos live in Africa. They live near lakes or rivers. The water must be deep enough for the hippos to **submerge** themselves. If a hippo is out of the water too long, its skin will become dry. The skin will start to crack.

FUN FACT

The word *hippopotamus* means "river horse" in Greek.

CHAPTER 2

LARGE AND ROUND

Hippopotamuses are huge **mammals**. A hippo can be approximately 12 feet (3.7 m) long. It can weigh approximately 6,500 pounds (2,948 kg). Male hippos are larger than females.

> A hippo's body is large and round.

A hippo sticks its head out of the water.

A hippo's thick skin is brownish gray. The skin on their bellies is pink in color. Hippos' bodies are almost hairless. But they have stiff whiskers on their upper lips. They also have hair on their ears and on their tails.

Hippos have four **webbed** toes on each foot. They spend a lot of time in the water. The webbing helps the animal move in water. It also keeps the hippo from falling when it walks on slippery riverbanks.

Hippos can open their mouths very wide.

FUN FACT

A hippo's teeth can reach lengths of
20 inches (51 cm).

Hippos have small ears. But their
jaws are enormous. Inside their
mouths are big teeth and **tusks**.
Tusks are long teeth.

Hippos can be aggressive. They
will fight animals they see as
threats. They sometimes fight other
hippos, too. When fighting, they
often use their teeth and tusks.

CHAPTER 3

MADE FOR WATER

Hippos often rest with most of their bodies under the water. But they can still see everything around them. Hippos' eyes are high on their heads. This lets them see even when they are submerged.

 Hippos spend most of their day in the water.

A hippo underwater

A hippo's eyes have clear **membranes**, too. These cover the hippo's eyes when it goes underwater. The hippo can see. The membranes protect its eyes.

Hippos' nostrils are high on their heads, too. The nostrils also close when the animal goes underwater.

Hippos can sleep in water. When they need to breathe, they rise to the surface for air. Then they sink back to the bottom until they need to breathe again. They never wake up during this process.

FUN FACT

Hippos can hold their breath underwater for up to five minutes.

PARTS OF A HIPPOPOTAMUS

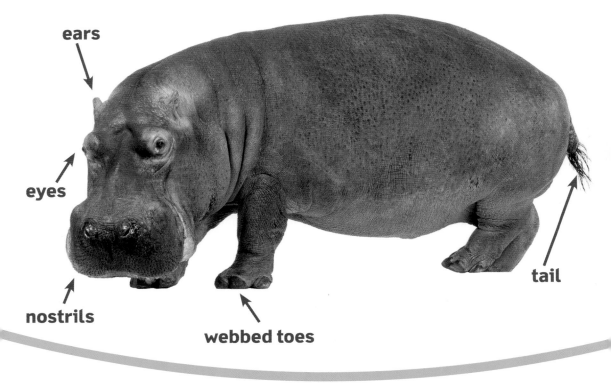

ears

eyes

nostrils

webbed toes

tail

Hippos can run surprisingly fast for their size. In short distances, they can run as fast as a human being. Hippos can reach speeds of

A group of hippos run into the water.

14 miles per hour (23 km/h). This can help them escape **predators**. They run into the water, where they are safe. However, hippos cannot swim. They move through the water quickly by pushing themselves off other objects.

SPECIAL SKIN

Hippos **secrete** an oily red substance. It comes from the animal's sweat glands. For many years, people wondered what this odd liquid was. Hippos are the only animals that produce it. At first, scientists thought it might be sweat. But careful testing showed that it was not. Scientists now think the substance is a natural **antibiotic**. This means the liquid helps prevent infections. Experts think it also acts as a sunscreen for the animal's sensitive skin.

Staying in the water helps a hippo's skin by keeping it moist.

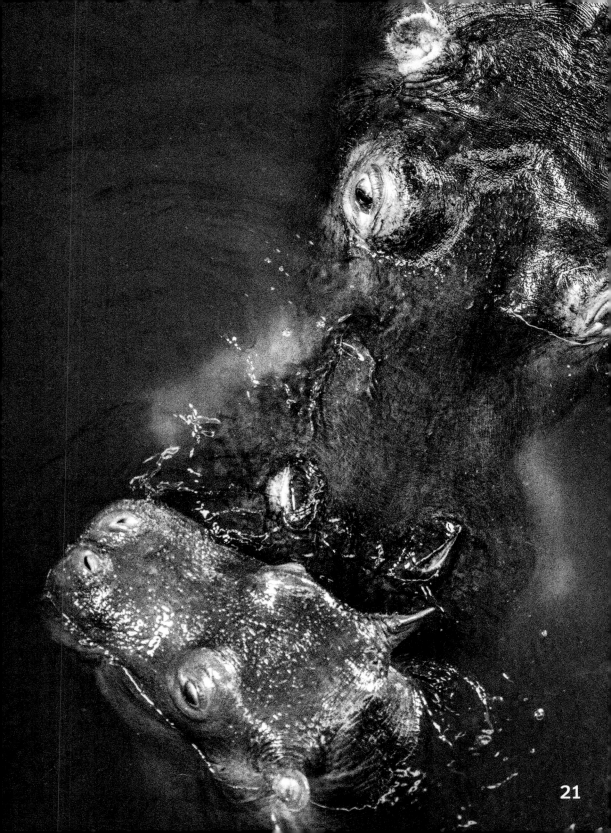

CHAPTER 4

DON'T GET IN THEIR WAY!

Hippopotamuses are highly **social** animals. They spend their time in groups. These are called schools. Each school has between 10 and 30 members. One male hippo leads each school.

Hippos live in large groups.

HIPPO LIFE CYCLE

A female has one calf at a time.

A calf weighs approximately 100 pounds (45 kg) at birth.

The oldest, strongest male leads the group.

Male hippos are called bulls. Females are called cows. Cows have one newborn every two years. It is called a calf. Calves may drink their mothers' milk on land. They can also close their ears and nostrils to nurse underwater.

After a calf is born, the school surrounds it. The hippos do this to protect the calf from predators. A hippo's predators are crocodiles, hyenas, and lions.

Hippos usually look for food at night.

Hippos are **herbivores**. They eat mostly grass. They can eat 80 pounds (36 kg) of grass in a single night. Hippos also eat fruit. But they do not need to eat every day. Hippos can go three weeks without eating. They can store food in their stomachs.

FOCUS ON
HIPPOPOTAMUSES

Write your answers on a separate piece of paper.

1. Write a sentence that explains the main idea of Chapter 2.

2. Which trait do you think is most useful to a hippo? Why?

3. How far might a hippo travel in one night while searching for food?

    A. 6 miles (10 km)

    B. 10 miles (16 km)

    C. 17 miles (27 km)

4. What might happen if a school of hippos thinks a person is going to harm them?

    A. The hippos will look for food.

    B. The hippos will attack.

    C. The hippos will stand perfectly still.

5. What does **aggressive** mean in this book?

*Hippos can be **aggressive**. They will fight animals they see as threats.*

    A. soft and gentle

    B. very smart

    C. ready to attack

6. What does **nurse** mean in this book?

*Calves may drink their mothers' milk on land. They can also close their ears and nostrils to **nurse** underwater.*

    A. to eat plants for food

    B. to be fed milk

    C. to clean oneself

Answer key on page 32.

GLOSSARY

antibiotic
A substance that kills germs.

forage
To search for food.

herbivores
Animals that eat mostly plants.

mammals
Animals that give birth to live babies, have fur or hair, and produce milk.

membranes
Thin layers of tissue found in animals or plants.

predators
Animals that hunt other animals for food.

secrete
To release something through the skin.

social
Likely to spend time with other animals of the same type.

submerge
To become covered with water.

webbed
Having skin that connects the toes.

TO LEARN MORE

BOOKS

Diaw, Boris. *Hoops to Hippos!: True Stories of a Basketball Star on Safari*. Washington, DC: National Geographic, 2015.

Murray, Julie. *Hippopotamuses*. Minneapolis: Abdo Publishing, 2012.

Shea, Therese M. *20 Fun Facts About Hippos*. New York: Gareth Stevens, 2012.

NOTE TO EDUCATORS

Visit **www.focusreaders.com** to find lesson plans, activities, links, and other resources related to this title.

INDEX

A
Africa, 7

C
calf, 24, 25

E
eyes, 15, 16

F
females, 9, 24, 25
fight, 13, 24
food, 7, 27

G
groups, 23, 24

L
length, 9

M
males, 9, 23, 24, 25

N
nostrils, 17, 25

P
predators, 25

R
run, 18–19

S
skin, 7, 11, 20
sleep, 17

T
toes, 11
tusks, 13

W
water, 6–7, 11, 15, 16–17, 19
weight, 9